PETER LEVI · VIRIDITAS

PETER LEVI

Viriditas

ANVIL PRESS POETRY

Published in 2001
by Anvil Press Poetry Ltd
Neptune House 70 Royal Hill London SE10 8RF

Copyright © Deirdre Levi 2001

This book is published with financial assistance
from The Arts Council of England

Designed and set in Monotype Bell by Anvil
Printed and bound in England
by Cromwell Press, Trowbridge, Wilts

ISBN 0 85646 351 0

A catalogue record for this book
is available from the British Library

FOR BISHOP PETER WALKER

CONTENTS

PREFACE

THESE LAST POEMS were written in the shadows of
Peter's increasing blindness, an effect of diabetes,
although he never completely lost all sight. The condi-
tion is awkward to describe, sight being somehow from
round the sides of the eyes, so that he could see trees
and buildings better than people, who might often
appear to him with no heads. He missed seeing the
stars. He could not, however, read at all during his last
two years, however magnified the letters, so these
poems he mostly scribbled out, not being able to read
them through. Then they were transcribed by a friend,
Dot Jackson, after deciphering and dictation. Dot also
came once a week to read poetry to him, and he listened
to tapes. The last poem he heard was T. S. Eliot reading
'Ash Wednesday'.

These last poems are mostly local, as Peter very
much enjoyed walking round the village green, on his
own, with stick and small dog, stopping often for
conversation. This is a very watery place (in the
Berkeley Vale, flat land wedged between the edge of the
Cotswolds and the Forest of Dean) with the river
Severn across several large fields dotted with horses;
and near to the village the Gloucester and Sharpness
canal, lively with boats and occasionally the tall ships.
The beautiful green of 22 acres has three large ponds,
and around the village are several lakes formed from
gravel pits. Aeroplanes are seldom heard, but instead
flying swans and formations of geese. There are a good
many cormorants and herons, and plenty of larks and
curlews. Peacocks roam freely.

DEIRDRE LEVI

Frampton-on-Severn, March 2001

THE ICY BANK has settled down to drink
among trees, black water runs into the sea,
the sun also declines like the last sun
dying among the cavernous ribs of Wales.

So WHEN we got up late out of our beds
the frost was nearly melted from the green,
the sun was gilding our white window-bars
and streaked the apples on the window-sills.
Trees fingered the grass with a darkness:
receding hoofbeats and birds yammering
like a long weekend between year and year.
I cannot remember if we are alive
but for the rattle of clockwork in my skull
saying Too late. You are drowning in sleep,
other poets shake it off like shadows.

LATE IN the night I saw, clear in my sight,
the comet swim like a pink bee in light.

[I]

IN THE FRESH forest wandering and lost:
where birdwings flutter and the shadows hang
early the sun from the green covert sprang
and the tall sky clarified and storm-tossed.
The roadside had broken into a surf of white
under the oak trees dripping down mustiness of green,
and on the forest floor the climbing ferns repine
and the small birds lament, the birds entreat.
We were most lost when we each other found
like that green sea that shatters on the rocks
in silver green and golden natural shocks
melting away at sunset with no sound
in mere perspiring and pure natural breath,
shadows in shadows, and the last is death.

[II]

Two POLES twirling and trembling north to south
whizzing and wobbling in a sea of light
like spheres of fire for ever out of sight,
or like two rivers spouting mouth to mouth,
two springs of ocean, under one sea floor
greening each other's water breast to breast
freezing into one sunset and cold west
and yet still pouring as green oceans pour
as ragged birds pour on through the night sky
and moonlight pours between the mist and cloud,
and high above the wind you hear the loud
concerted creak as Russian swans go by:
we are two oceans, and our breath is single,
and our souls only live when our fires mingle.

[III]

LONG LONELY bones of the Siberian swan
turn to ice sculpture in the freezing gale
yet they fly on like ice-ships that can sail
cold waters after long winter's begun,
and the wolf howls for hunger near his death,
trees crack and fall and axes on the ice ring:
that is no time for human travelling,
the frosted woods make ice of animal breath:
and now the swans have gone far overhead,
and happy is the young man whose hot blood
can dream beyond ice caverns and mere food
to summon up a lover to his bed.
We breed, accommodating as we may
the turning of the season and the day.

[IV]

THERE IS a spring that can never return,
unforeseen, unmated, unnatural,
when the wind hums in the pine forest and all
deep scented roses in the garden burn.
How often now in sleep we wander there
and choose to sleep for meeting when we wake
dizzy with gardens and the dazzling lake,
and wander dazed through the life we live here:
the bare downs and the rhetoric of stone,
silver-grey rococo and vast baroque
where rivers croon in underlying rock
and we always together, always alone
withering down in one bed to one ghost
are in fresh forest wandering and lost.

WHEN WE were young we dreamed we'd grow to be
like guardian spirits in the Muses' wood,
but those who walk the tracks of poetry
seldom come to much good.

SOMETIMES you listen to a far-off noise
and wonder and muse and wait
until you shiver like the night-time trees:
How did it get so late?

THE NORMAL boy runs to the training ground:
those who are not trot where they are not found,
they fade into the ground
without a sound.

The normal boy who nothing will astound
has direct eyes, those who are not look round
at the far edge of the ground
without a sound.

The normal man pays his way pound for pound,
those who are not valued, not sound,
and they fear the cold ground,
hares fear the hound.

The old diminish, but they still abound
in normal pleasures: as for the unsound
they have gone from the ground
without a sound.

STAGNUM

RAIN DRIPPING from the darkening green trees:
a smell of garlic ruined in the green woods
and stink of horsepiss on the stable walls.
There is something stagnant about my poetry,
all my life reduces to stagnant water,
dark, weedy, unreflective of the sun.
It is a stagnation, or consider
our dog, the murmured pleasure of his dreams
among dog-blankets, far inside the mind:
he is lost in cavern beyond cavern.
It may be heaven is my labyrinth,
or that this dead water lapped heaven once:
which has stagnated here in the reed-beds
where I will that my ashes be scattered.

LYME REGIS

SEASIDE hotel, bath in the wall's thickness
rooms regency, unrevived,
Chevaux de Marly in the dining-room.
George Snell bred racing pigeons
for the Resistance which was to come.
Over the road a hundred years old
an old man of a hundred
among the swallows under the reed roof
with an eye open for his grandmother.
Quacker owts an sowt biskuts
an a clean loif, he said.

SHADE TREES, monument of old shadows,
I am overshadowed now with fresh shadow,
in the white intricacies of a rose.

THE TREES are standing in a field of mist
and in a long field of their own shadows
sun breaks through into intense light-green
making the trees tower enlace enclose
all that is left of grass smells and shadow.

WE OLD MEN float like feathers down the green
anchored to earth by dim eyes like torch-light,
this is the time when puppies cannot smell
because the willow-herb has gone to seed:
noses block with white drift, they smell nothing
but gambol, frisk and look at you sad-eyed.
They are too young, we are too old for school,
for them just to run wild is heaven's gift,
we sit below a wall and pause a while
in the soft sun while the sun is burning,
is burning and turning, never returning.

BARROW HILL

BLACK-EYED vicunas that outstare the moon
have cropped the white clover from Barrow Hill
as if they might have come
out of the Roman forest and the Welsh stone
where Severn wrinkles till millennium:
the shepherd does not know America or Rome,
the flock is far from home
and Caesar's elephant dwindles to shadow.

Lay down in shelter of Buffon's green tree
upstream of Paris, under his green plane
so gentle that they can't
be pushed beyond that limit they give free
or they'll despair and die in their meek pain:
let the Jardin des Plantes stand for their monument
like shadows they live on
and rational Buffon
must grieve for their lost innocent continent.

Because there is weight and wealth in the mountain
slave beast and peasant hauling through the rains,
Buffon had read in Bolivar,
herded from grazing grounds and lost ruins
three hundred thousand llamas worked the mines
by roads so hard and far
the mind dizzies and falls,
there was no one to care
how they died in despair
by battering their own heads on the rock walls.

Mysterious estuary or underworld
of Charon where fires crackle in the gloom
and sainted animals
pass clover hills and the mountains are cold:
yet one bowl of peaches will scent a room
and never a leaf falls,
until mist covers all
that the dying eye sees of intimate faces:
twittering till the trumpet cracks the ball.

Day droops, the distant wailing dies away
then the whole estuary is one blaze
gleam of dissolving suns,
all the debris of every day,
our Cocytus, our flames of Phlegethon
which interfusing runs
nine times around like doom,
framing the last we see:
some lovely Greek maybe,
some oiled and unknown face from the Fayyum.

We have wasted our will's power too long
on rock and heath and paintings of hill-sides
white page and sketching board
where the whole visible world sells for a song
and soul like any grazing llama feeds
on moons of white cardboard
not bruised by the white cloud
by rain or river-spray
that might have washed away
our unclean history where we cried aloud.

EARLY AUGUST: roses rot in the rain
the old dullness comes rustling down again
under the garden wall
white petals drift and fall.

Village borders are mauve and yellow now,
ragged bungalow hedges, rank shadow,
the mothy time of year
has settled in I fear.

There is no hope in the old moon or new moon,
the tractors rumble by all afternoon,
I sense the earliest dumb
wish that winter will come.

WHEN MILTON climbed up into heaven at last
God had become an old Jewish refugee,
or tweedily retired into the west
to that last gazebo under a ruined tree,
fuming with malt whisky and with sunset,
or like a worn-out spy raising chickens
with too much information and sore feet,
reluctant to discuss the might have been.
Let Milton worry what God has become
and whether or not he believes in it,
let Tolstoy puff and blow at heaven like steam,
God is in the long queue of shuffling feet
whose comfort is music, whose eyes are blind,
he has not got new Americas in mind.

THE LONG buzz of the aromatic bee
has infected this afternoon's lavender bush:
shadows of iron crumbled to poetry
and heaven echoing earth in one blue wash.

An essence that the alchemist distilled,
crystalline, unctuous, brewed from an acorn,
that might have overtopped this tree and filled
the blue with buzzings too tired to be born.

No MOUNTAINS, and you cannot see the hills
but the blue mist is shaking with machines,
a tremble and mutter that somehow fills
our senses as we sicken in the plains,
which were a labyrinth of mystery,
chessboard of little squares lined with elm trees:
now all the hedges are misted cloud high,
and one tea-rose clings on and sighs and dies.

UNDER FROCESTER HILL

[I]

MID AUGUST: Mary's fair on the cricket grass
lights up at dusk until the midnight air
fizzes the Malvern water in a glass:
fireweed and fireworks and the sky on fire:
and only here in this obscurest place,
claypits, river-marsh, fox-holes, gravel-holes
that saw the body of King Edward pass
and heard the heron's cry for drowning souls:
of all England we hold this fair and feast
tied to St. Mary's and her mystery:
how she rose like a vision from her death
into the long swoon of the kiss of Christ,
spiring up high like the fireweeds we can see,
high as the heaven of heavens in God, in faith.

[II]

The prehistoric stones nuzzled like sheep
in the long grass round about Frocester hill
and the heat gathered most where there was a deep
shade under hedges and songbirds were still.
Long ago the reform has come and gone,
but here the Virgin is lifted up high
and the old bell chanted his iron tone,
she is like a firework in flower in the sky
trailing her country beauties into heaven
only from this parish, why no one knows,
but this one day is not quite forgotten,
and still under this tree hangs heaven's rose,
and the sheep graze and stones graze on blue air:
so come to the fair children, come to the fair.

[III]

A BRIMMING moon so yellow and so white
it turned the conifers as black as iron:
a Japanese print, colour made of light
and the sky blown away for a new one.
The fair had shaken off its old music
and spun into a wildness of delight
one pink green yellow whizz of fantastic
electric architecture boiled green-bright,
great beams rising and falling suspended
never engulfed, sweeping like demon brushes,
forest madness or last news of the dead
sweeping off foliage and fantasies:
we are too far gone, I cannot imagine
the Virgin mother and Moon-queen in this heaven.

PERCEPTION

WEEPING and melting from a crust of ice
and hurling headlong into frozen light
with a roar down a hundred foot rock-face
in one white ribbon so unearthly bright
it plays among rainbows riding on air
to dissolve into water-mist as it falls,
dying out in transparent diamond fire
and the wet glisten of the rocky walls,
yet fills the green seas with continuous streams
and is from snow to sea one element
as dark is with the coloured fires of dreams
or the jackdaws in crowish discontent
seem one music, one babble of stones on stones,
or dribble of dove-tones down afternoons.

FOR C. C. 80

CHARLES as the pebble in the tinkling stream
High on the moor where it breaks from the granite
And trickles down among moss-weeds that gleam
Rough among bogs and so cold and so bright,
Light as a dream-poem
Exact as flight,
Stone-cold as stone, you are the stone in them.

Charles, there is no boundary any more
And the business of verse building has gone over,
Unless that plot where your roses still soar
Shyer than children every year appear:
Live for a century,
End the old year
You planted, be as poems can be, free.

THE LOOSE trees grazing in the park
against a ground of Lincoln green
uncovered, but the fields were dark
and August leaves were limp and lean.

It was the shadow between leaves
that made the evening trees look dark,
it is the lighted sky that heaves
the sunlight high above the park

dropping shade between leaf and leaf
until the hills of green we see
seem shadow-dunes, and heights of life
go black as walls, tree after tree.

URASHIMA

*[Penguin Basho p. 152, n. 11, and R. Acad. Hiroshigi
Catalogue 1977]*

LEAN SPINE of island, stars antique
but cold and merely silver-gilt,
over the sea-sand where they seek
for drips of light the moon has spilt

and gather it into sea-shells
to carry it away with night
so that a moss of moonlight fills
the sea's face in one dazzling sheet.

Then at sunrise when the fresh sun
first blazes up out of the east
the dry sea-sand will break open
and young sea-turtles be released

from the warm sand to the bright light
to swim in their own element
as the sun climbs hoary and bright
above the roof of their blue tent.

There passed a lonely fishing boy
loitering homeward silently,
when the year's turtles with one cry
all flung themselves into the sea.

It was the blazing of the sun
that drew them from their broken shells,
that glittering magnetic stone
millions of miles away who feels

the turtle crying in the sand,
and in one moment they are gone,
but the boy could not understand
how one was blind and left alone.

And now with probing, curving beak
the wild birds that cry out by day
were combing in the sand to seek
whatever might flounder astray.

The boy had seen the blinded eyes
and took the turtle in his hand,
left the sea-birds and their wild cries
to broken egg-shells and dry sand.

No fishing boy was ever bolder
or so compassionate as he
taking the turtle on his shoulder
ran out into the lisping sea.

The turtle would not go from him,
he swam beyond the sight of sail
among the dolphin-shoals and dim
sea-regions of the humming whale.

Suddenly it was noon, there rose
a spinning wave of purple sea
crowned with sea-foam that flew and froze
soaring into the sun's bright eye,

it wrapped then round in one dark fold
of the deep water of the sea,
vast purple skin gleaming with gold
as it sank back into the sea.

It was not drowning, but the wave
roared in their ears, and the immense
sea reared to save as the sea can save
shell beyond sounding shell of sense,

spiralling downwards, drowning star
or inward labyrinth of shell,
and swiftest of all things that are
turtle and boy together fell

into a green and silver light
an unknown world of freshest air,
a heaven dripping cool and bright,
a palace, a vermilion chair.

There sat the goddess of the sea
who took the turtle in her hands
and the boy breathed, and laughed and he
knelt down upon the damp sea-sands,

where weeds in green and purple state
slowly fanning the peacock hair
looked glossier and more delicate
for breathing that star-silver air,

and oceanic green in play
rose fountains from the coral rock,
far out of sight to fall in spray,
so all the air glimmered and shook.

Goddesses naked without shame
and gods like aged fishermen
called Urashima by his name
to come and play with their children,

while animals of the deep sea
revelled or slunk without a sound,
the sea-wasp danced with the ocean-bee
quietly over holy-ground

and yellow leaf and crimson fruit
climbed by slow ages from the sand
scenting the gardens with delight
and dropping ripe into the hand.

He played what seemed a summer's day
though no sun rose for him or set,
bowed his goodbyes and saw his way,
and dived where the wave's back was wet

and spiralled upwards like a star
or inward labyrinth of shell
into the sun and the blue air
and on the sudden sand he fell.

But not one boat was riding there,
and where the bamboo roofs had been
there was no cottage and no fire,
and the roof beam had fallen in.

Then he opened a silver box
the sea-goddess had given him,
weeping and crying to the rocks,
and wept until his eyes grew dim.

Out of it rose a twist of smoke
twisting up like the spinning wool,
a thing that alters while you look
and his beard grew down white and full.

He tells his story, and he sighs
and weeps as he tells it again,
and waits for the full moon to rise,
old man sitting among old men.

THE GREAT trees shake
their vast shadows
thousands of leaves
endless concertos,

all day as bright
as Sion's meadows,
and dark all night
as neon shadows.

The rigmaroles
of leaf and summer
and moonlit miles
will soon be over.

THE JUICES break out of the ground
into the greenness of the trees,
far overhead as if crow-caws
and harmonies of surf could reach
yellow pressings of plum or peach.

The spirit of earth leaps out to fly
beyond all boundaries and shake
out music, as a bird might break
the perfect eggshell of the sky.

ISLANDS in the mist in the dark estuaries:
gold hands of time just touch them like a clock
where the sea blackens but it will not freeze,
they gleam bright green but smell as sweet as smoke.
Far away from this world they must appear
like the star-dust of crushed constellations
but here while the sun reigns and they look near,
sheep-houses, whale-harbours or steamer-stations,
gleaming and quiet, ruin beyond ruin
time hardly touching, sun scarcely present,
how islanded by mist to wander in,
and the rough waves that mouth this continent.

LUR

OF DENMARK I recall
only the hollow sour
hoot of an antique horn
made on a forest floor,
a mossy brazen call
re-echoed, blowing down
prehistory, as cold
and futile as the dawn.

SEASON OF THE HERMIT

IT IS seven in the morning
and he is still a hermit of ground-mist
at noon the sun is shining
and an apple-tree's coldness is all his feast,
the water-springs run for repentance
down from his rocky eyes,
all afternoon notes the season's advance,
and the wood-birds ingeminating peace.
September now, before a leaf falls
at evening when the foliage is ripe
and far away the barn-owl calls
over his dripping pillow he will sleep.

IN MEMORY OF TURCIUS RUFUS
APRONICUS ASTERIUS, CONSUL 494

IN 500 AD
Germans settled like flies
on southern Italy,
vigorous with blue eyes.

They ate at new tables
made of one long plank,
like horses in their stables
or like soldiers in ranks

they lived on sausages,
their rubbish was pig-bones,
they dumped all at their ease
by front doors and hearth stones:

they feasted happily
inside the Roman farms,
and sang in ecstasy
of ancestors and arms.

Meanwhile with patient skill
an old consul took care
to copy out Virgil
as fine as his white hair.

Now I MUST climb high up the wooden and white
stairway above the brick comfort of this house,
above learning, above poetry, above sight,
to gather thoughts like birds and let them loose,
shadow hunt shadow till the hunt goes right
and then these stoop on those.

Though it is only shadow-poetry:
I recall your real poems, your real tones,
the shelly trumpet grumbling distantly,
the sea-grind of the light, sea-groan of bones,
honoured among the dazzle still to be,
honoured among sea-stones.

THE SEA slumbers in grottoes of dark stone:
in metallic blinks or flash of fainting light
shepherds dark water into dark withdrawn
and if you shine a torch it washes white
on grotesque walls that whisper on and on
in one long nightmare where there is no sight
the sleepy mind rests in itself alone
with colours folded in the bed still bright,
the sea heaves downwards like a telephone
to speak of nothing, things beneath its feet,
till the old stones break open in a yawn
and the sea settles, waves are curled up tight,
daybreak warm with the moaning of the bone
floats from the grottoes like a paper kite.

FOR LEOPARDI

FOR POETRY you need only a room
like a leaf dropping quietly from a tree,
tranquillities of lamplight far from home:
I have been lucky to find them certainly,
despair beyond the gothicry of gloom,
beyond philosophy.

I remember your window high on the house walls
and have recalled it twenty or thirty years,
last poet and last classic whose line appals
this bleakness of our paper death that bears
a shallow leaf, a fruit that falls
into blushing and tears.

FOR ROSE

AMONG SO many there is always one
rose that will live and die most like the sun,
dense-leaved, dark-hearted and sweet-skinned like one
that is wet with the mild dew of the moon.

Now MAUVE and mothlike the still petals hang
in green and aspen shivers
dropping a shower of yellow leaf
mysterious noises of mountain rivers:
continuous and visionary grief,
elm or black poplar where the wild bird sang
that year by year returning to this place
made music of generations
all summer screened but loudly heard
over sheep-runs grazed with antique patience,
slow congregation fed without a word
on meadows across the earth's green face.

THE EQUINOCTIAL gales bellowed and passed,
we slide into the long nights and the dark days
woods sicken and the leaves fall away fast
the vixen runs through ground-mist and moon haze

it was the darkened mornings taught the Muse
daily to come to Milton blind in his bed,
no bird-chorus nor summer's air confuse
that chanting, tranquil water-song of the dead.

So the moon melts away, the planet turns,
heaven's fire grazes my neighbour's roof-top,
only towards morning one bright star burns
while hollow caverns of the earth fill up.

DIMANCHE:
Les pommiers de la Manche,
Pommes vapeur.

FREESIAS butter-yellow on the sill.
The milk-white dog is rolling on this rug.
Make honey deeper coloured than the rug
from the green sap still running in Virgil.

Ice melted, the sun pressed
under crimson in the west,
high aeroplanes left furrows red
in the sky blue faded.
Frosty morning tree shadows
green and white, green hardly shows.
The swan that never sings
whizzing his wings.
The blue air quivered after him
and somewhere in the mist a dim
wood-pigeon cried cuckoo.
Cuckoo, cuckoo.

THE FALLS go spinning down into the woods
out of a grove of laurel, that sweet smell,
of cliffs of rock and in among the trees.

Virgil, AENEID 6.658–9

GASLIGHT LIKE the soft jaws of crocodiles,
Postcards carried from county to county
Scribbled in tea-shops with small messages.
The empire was dying of boredom.
The shirts lay quiet in chest of drawers,
On Mondays they were frisking in the wind
And all the kitchens smelt of ironing.
The age of guns, oil cans and bicycles,
Shire horses like cathedrals pulled haystacks,
And paddle-steamers splashed in the sea-spray,
A trail of coloured postcards in their wake.
The fainting skies curdled like cream and roses,
Spring time of birds a hundred years ago.

UNDER THE GREEN water beaded with silver
plunges the otter streaking like a diver
into the mystery of his dark chamber
to rest in hay colours and tones of amber.

Thunder touches the edge of the long hills
and down the grass edges rain spills
to Severn water now only the sun's ember
glimmers in caves and riverfalls of amber.

The otter sleeps to wake when the moon rises
to swim as the moon swims or as the night pleases
sinking through pool and watery falls of umber
to surface in green reeds with eyes of amber.

THE RAGGED SWAN was hissing like a kettle
the stream was green and murky as a bottle
ruffling the water with his clear white breast
where the trees laid down their heads to rest.

More venomous than any English snake
and spewing pure malice poising to strike
he was weaving with fury, to see someone, anyone
kebabed, skewered, with all their guts undone.

It was the fox that burrowed in the night
to murder cygnets before their coats were white
silently before blood was in the sky
and robbed the swan's nest when the moon was high.

SILENCE BEFORE it thunders, hardly a sigh
heaves in heaven not a tree murmurs
not a squirrel skitters over the dead leaves,
not a fieldmouse stirs.

The heavy patter of the early drops
and the first thunder growls or it murmurs
and for one moment the world's machinery stops,
not a fieldmouse stirs.

Thunder and rain no sound of any bird,
the rain increased there was no sound to be heard
only the rain on the black poplar murmured
but not a fieldmouse stirred.

THE EELS are running now, the meadows drown
the woods in river water upside down
in rivers stand as still as any stone
dark images that never can be mown.

Now trailing her dark hours the night falls
the slight leaf shivers and the last bird calls
until the sky hangs down his blackened walls
as the most ancient kings their funerals.

Now the young foxes in the silence play
only the tall moon's bland and freakish eye
watches on what dark feet the hours go by
and death itself seems nothing but a sigh.

Rose-hips and blackberries fresh on the branch
mark autumn stepping out into the hush
of summer's heavy dews and dying wish,
till the world shivers and begins to drench.

It is the time for silence and for storms
and for the bright waves crumbling round our shores,
time for the puzzled dog digging old bones
and robins in the ruined apple cores.

The weather is off balance, only silence
is spreading around us like a season,
it is the season of some inward sense
as the wind drones on with an inward tone.

THERE WAS book-learning, my lost powers,
and religion once in an ocean of grass:
now wings creak in the withering sky, birds swim
    in glass
and I can taste the stones of ruined towers.

The poems die away to housedust on the tongue
their season is like death, it will not return
out of that darkness where the starlight burns,
out of the dead gardens and the times' distress.

No matter I suppose, because night will fall,
just one old poet wandering along the world's edge
fingering the dead strings for the moon's old
        privilege
and the lake's surface for its last bird-calls.

OVER THE WALL where the ivy was
and the bee is buzzing in the ivy still
and only the scent and the silence fill
the last of the blue air and the sun's pause
as it goes down.

How perfect the last touch of daylight is
until the shadows stretch across the green
and no bees are anywhere to be seen
and all the world will settle down to freeze
when the sun is gone.

SHEEP and the ground mist and the river-noise:
some kind of oil has rubbed from the moon
and stained the fleeces and the standing stone
before it floated free to the moon-rise
above the tall stone and the taller trees.

The sheep are dark now since the moon rose
they gleam a moment silvery and bright
but shadow beyond shadow they repeat
the same dark formula to the sky's height
drying their wet fleece in the river-breeze.

Yet if the moon is hidden we are dark
and the great owl sweeps on enormous wings
out of the forest after nameless things
she cries and terrifies till sheep look stark
breathing their panic where the shadows walk.

WHAT ARE the old men muttering in the park?
There are no children playing:
the sun has gone and it is getting dark
they wear long overcoats, the trees are swaying,
what are they saying?

They shuffle home soon they will all be dead,
not a bird is left.
The birds have said what needed to be said
house lights glimmer and seem bereft
of the years we have lived.

There is no wind breathing over the lake
the angel has no trumpet and no voice
we are left brooding over an old mistake
There is something in us that had no choice
something that wants to lose.

MY OLD brown coat for the year's shortest days
with the wind coming icy out of Wales
when the sun has hardly the energy to rise
and slowly down the river pools he sails.

Now snow is on the Malverns and Manhattan
glitters from the loop line like Samarkand
the painted planes whirl like a carousel,
while here the snow lies crisp over the land.

But room by room I can hear waterfalls
loose from their pictures with a roar of doom.
I take my shoes off and I sigh downstairs
but hear them echoing from room to room.

IT IS the perfect weather
for the swan to shake his feather
but now on grass or green
the swan is nowhere seen
he is far from all alarms
among the silver palms

THE PSALMS

How SLOWLY now they seem to drag and ring
the wing flap of the spirit seems to flag
and nothing but the ghosts or shadows cling
high up like tattered remnants of some flag.

Yet I have seen the flag fly in bright air
and heard these tunes when they were magical
then fruit fell from ripe boughs till trees were bare
only white architecture could not fall.

Now it has fallen and the sky will fall
and the poems of Horace will come roaring down
the sphere of earth crumbles the heart of all
and psalms and choir music are winding down.

January 17 2000

Some Recent Poetry from Anvil

Oliver Bernard
Verse &c.

Nina Bogin
The Winter Orchards

Martina Evans
All Alcoholics Are Charmers

Michael Hamburger
Intersections

James Harpur
Oracle Bones

Anthony Howell
Selected Poems

Marius Kociejowski
Music's Bride

Gabriel Levin
Ostraca

Thomas McCarthy
Mr Dineen's Careful Parade

Stanley Moss
Asleep in the Garden

Dennis O'Driscoll
Weather Permitting

Sally Purcell
Fossil Unicorn

Peter Scupham
Night Watch

Daniel Weissbort
What Was All the Fuss About?